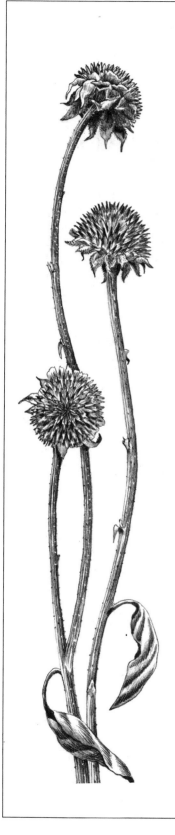

NATURE *notes*

DRAWINGS BY
MARGARET O'BRIEN
&
TEXT BY
URSULA SHEPHERD

a notebook companion
to the seasons

FULCRUM PUBLISHING

Library of Congress Cataloging-in-Publication Data

Shepherd, Ursula L., 1946–
       Nature notes : a notebook companion to the seasons /
Ursula L. Shepherd and Margaret O'Brien.
       p.   cm.
       ISBN 1-55591-056-4
1. Nature Study, 2. Seasons. 3. diaries (Blank-books)
I. O'Brien, Margaret, 1948–   II. Title.
Qh51.S49 1990
508—dc20   89-29529
CIP

Fulcrum Publishing
350 Indiana Street
Suite 510
Golden, CO 80401

Printed in the United States of America
10 9 8 7 6 5 4 3 2 1

Book Design by AnnW. Douden

CONTENTS

PREFACE

This book is crafted by two who come to the love of nature and the use of field notes from different directions, yet it is those differences that make it easy for each of us to see and understand the strengths of the other. Margy O'Brien is first a painter and I am first a writer, and we each strive to be naturalists. We have found that our love of nature carries over into, and defines, the art each of us practices.

We met over skeletons in zoology class. In lab we were required to keep notebooks. Margy drew what she needed to remember. I recorded meticulous notes. Although each of us had spent much time outdoors with a notebook, neither of us had had any experience with a field journal that focused entirely on nature and that incorporated both writing and sketching. But the second class we took together required that we start one. On class field trips we learned, tentatively at first, to use those journals. Then we began to take trips of our own.

As we spent more and more time in the field, writing and drawing through the seasons, we began to recognize the special relationship with nature that our books nurtured. Margy began to write, and I, having assured myself I couldn't sketch, began to do just that, turning shades of light and dark over in my mind as I put pencil to paper. In merging the two forms, we each learned more about the other's craft—and about the natural world.

I saw that one must stop and linger; nature's secrets don't reveal themselves in the sweep of a passing nod. Drawing slowed me down. I had to sit, whereas, before, I had walked and *thought* I saw—but hadn't. Margy concentrated on sharpening senses other than sight. To write meant she could record sounds and smells and tactile sensations as well as visual ones. In the process, nature's glory opened ever wider to both of us, and we each learned to be present in the moment in ways we had not known before. We then wanted to create a field journal that was beautiful yet functional and which, in some way, reflected our love of the time spent in the company of our own notebooks. Here it is.

—Ursula Shepherd

ACKNOWLEDGMENTS

Many people inspired us and helped us with this book. The first must surely be the three men who insisted we keep field notes for their classes and who shared with us their sheer wonder at the natural world: Dr. Jim Findley, Dr. Cliff Crawford and Dr. Manuel Molles.

Dr. David Hafner of the New Mexico Museum of Natural History read and critiqued portions of the manuscript and offered his encouragement. Greg Farley of the University of New Mexico read other segments. This book would not have been nearly so easy to write had we not had access to the various collections of the University of New Mexico Biology Department, where everyone was enthusiastic and generous with their time and comments.

Our editors, Pat Frederick and Betsy Armstrong, also deserve thanks for their insight and support. They saw the book as we did, and sometimes saw it better than we could. Their appreciation of our intent made this first book a delight for both of us.

And, of course, there are our husbands, Bill and Ken, who cooked many meals, often had their schedules disrupted, and put up with all sorts of inconvenience with nary a grumble. To both of them, our deep thanks.

INTRODUCTION

Artists fill sketchbooks; writers keep journals; and naturalists, whether professional or amateur, keep field notebooks. But who is a naturalist? Can you claim to be one? The dictionary defines a naturalist as one who studies natural objects such as plants, animals and minerals. Among the naturalist's primary skills are the ability to see and the ability to record—the skills most prized by the artist and the writer. One tool most encourages and enhances these abilities: the simple field journal. Unpretentious as it is, it acts as a keel to steady its user, to center attention on the things observed. Using it, the naturalist hones the skills of watching, listening, smelling, questioning and recording.

The chief attribute of a field notebook is that it be functional. It's meant to be carried on walks, to be tucked in a backpack for a month-long hike in the Sierras, even to be left by the kitchen window for taking notes on birds at the feeder. It must be suitable for sketching, pasting leaves or photos into, or describing things seen one afternoon beside the pond.

This is such a book. Designed as a year-long journal, it is meant to provide a place for the musings of the walker, the backyard dreamer, the amateur naturalist, the artist. Get it dirty; let it live; claim it as a friend who has earned those lovely wrinkles in time well spent together. Whether you use it for noting the appearance of a wildflower in the crack of a city sidewalk or the arrival of golden eagles at their nesting grounds, whether it never goes farther than the garden or is with you scaling the mountains of Nepal, this small book will harbor your memories as no other companion can.

Use it for both sketching and writing, for each has its place as a record. You can't draw a smell and no verbal description of a rare flower offers what a single illustration can. Representative entries from some of our own trips show how you might use this book:

slight breeze , 70° +
cirrus clouds to the west
cumulus clouds building up in east
clear overhead

7-12-88
10:30 am
Audubon Nature Center walk
7200'? elev.

Butterflies, ants, birds and wildflowers all vie for our attention but I'm searching for a shady spot to lie on my back and stare up at the summer sky. I find just the spot and get comfortable. Margy, like the bees and ants around us — keeps working. I watch the red ants at their work, hoping it will inspire me — but honestly this is the perfect day to nap among the lupine, the snakeweed and the phlox.

Why are the butterflies so small? Often, as many as ten bluish butterflies land on one small plant, then they rise and spread out only to come back together at another plant some minutes later.

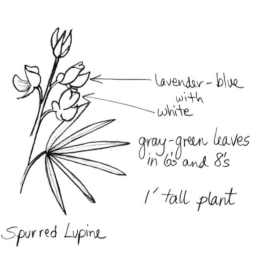

powder blue   copper   white with black dots

top   underneath

tiny butterfly — smaller than this drawing, feeding on 2 flowers, both similar in color:

smaller purple-blue flower clusters →

clover-type plant

2' tall plant

Alfalfa

lavender-blue with white

gray-green leaves in 6's and 8's

1' tall plant

Spurred Lupine

Here, beneath my tree I look out onto a grassy open area that slopes down toward the north — alfalfa rules the land — the ants work on, bees buzz nearby, and I drift off to sleep for just a moment in the sun.

Still a slight breeze
75° +
walking again

Spotted a perfect new
mushroom — whitish, barely
rosy-beige-tinted —
poking through the dirt
beside 1′ rock.

The rock is adorned with lichen — yellow-green, rusty orange,
gray-green and black. Sparkling mica finishes its finery.
The fungus proclaims the microhabitat this small rock
creates — at least along its downslope, north-facing side. There's
quartz strewn here and there but most of the rock is undisputed
red — iron? All around the rock are piñons and one
old juniper.

Higher up (8,000') in ponderosa pine zone — trees have changed now... piñons give way to ponderosas, one-seeded juniper to Rocky Mt. juniper. We found a whole group of mushrooms under a Rocky Mt. juniper.

blue-green "needles"

pointy, kinda droopy branching

Rocky Mt. Juniper

Wandered on to where the damp creek bed crosses the trail- here is an ecotone: riparian meets ponderosa pine.

Just a little further up the trail we spot the oddest plant I've ever seen. It's growing under pines.

The shade is dappled here - it's cool, the soil is dark & moist - ground is covered by bark & pine needles with grass coming up in straggly bits & pieces

We stop to look it up - can't find it - Margy draws it to identify later.

size ranged from 1"- 2½"

golden-tan

gold-colored really fine-textured spongy-looking instead of rays like previous one

yellowis "flowers

fleshy stalk 12"-18 with colored fuzz

PINEDROPS

When is a fungus a toadstool — when a mushroom?

2-25-88   12:30 pm
Cross-country ski trip- SANDIA CREST
                              RIM TRAIL
        alt. 10,000'
        40° F   No Wind

    Snow's been thin along the trail. Still icy in the shade but moving toward mush in the sun. We stopped and took off our skis at the edge of a small meadow. The day is bright, sunny and wispy shards of cloud meander across the sky. There's no wind, not even a breeze about. Once we stop it is silent — no sound but my pencil moving across the page.

    Is there any life about? Only plants and two humans - not even tracks in the snow nearby. I'm sitting under a "lichen tree" - old, double-trunked and gnarled. It's short and thick as are most of the trees that ring this spot. Do the winds cut more fiercely across this bit of crest? But what is it really, this tree? Cones turned down with tassals, needles that twist out of their bases — Douglas fir.

    A chirp! Is it a bird or squirrel? Red squirrel. I can't see it but he's chittering off to my left. How long has he been up? Somebody else is niggling in the distance — that's a bird but don't know which. Oops — there — Clark's Nutcracker.

    Snow drips from a tree across the meadow. I hear rather than see it. As I stop writing to listen I'm aware of the faintest ripple of a breeze.

    With hand lens - looked at the soft snow beside me. There are still distinct crystals even as it melts. Wish I could draw the prisms of colored light I see there, but I can't. Colors are yellow, green and purple.

    Winter is a snowy silent meadow — a crystal stillness. It's a day of sight and sound — in such stillness each sound is individual, sharp and true.

2-25-88
1:30 pm

alt. 10,000' 40°F No wind

Small meadow surrounded by
sub-alpine forest - Doug. fir, corkbark
fir, quaking aspen

the "Lichen Tree"

Sat here and drew for a couple of hours -
listened for life. There's more nubby coat
than needle to this tree. Two things appear
to live together - one clearly lichen, the
other maybe some fungus - or is it really
one in different forms? If two, how do
they live together?
Cones and needles high up - all
cones grow down. Needles blunt-tipped
come out singly from the bark. Shafts
twist - douglas fir

Why the double trunk?

What's this?

te lunch and
tened here -
Clark's Nutcracker
ied over us

"Old Man's Beard"
yellow-green color
fine-threaded
growing all over

break back on themse
look fluted like chante

Is this the fruit o
the fungal part of
the lichen?

Both drawing and writing are learned skills: you learn by doing. For the purposes of this book, don't be concerned about "doing it right" or producing a "work of art." This is not the time to make judgments about the quality of what you've put on the page. Begin with simple things—a leaf, for example. Leave behind your preconceived notions of what it's "supposed" to look like; instead, allow yourself to see as if for the first time.

With practice, drawing brings new understanding of an object and the parts that constitute it. In time, the link from eye to heart to hand will become more finely tuned and you'll gain skill in expressing what you want to convey about that leaf, shell, tree or cloudy sky. It may be the pattern of light and dark on a surface as it catches your eye; it may be a texture, an unusual angle, even the mood you feel at the moment. You may spend hours on a drawing or just make a quick jotting to help you identify an animal or plant from your reference books at home. Drawings record our response to nature in a way words cannot. A sketch, no matter how primitive or incomplete, helps us to see the intricacies of common subjects. Sketching keeps the vision fresh; it provides a different way to see.

Learning to write well is not so different from learning to draw. Demand no discipline, no inspiration, no formal technique. Relax. The value of a field journal lies in the spontaneity captured in the notations. Words work like the artist's lines; they are cues that represent the thing seen or smelled or felt. Let them tumble onto one another or stand separate. Don't force structure. Some observations will come as paragraphs, others as a jumble of words and phrases. Write simply. Write anything that enters your mind. Over time words will flow more freely.

Whether you write, or draw or simply record the morning's temperature, you will slow down. In this rushing, often mad-cap world there is a need for moments such as these. Take time out now and go for a walk. Go on! Try it out!

SPRING

Nature's calendar, unlike our own, begins with spring. One morning, a gray bird slowly folds its wings, brings its long, stilt legs forward and slips to earth. The great blue heron has returned to nest at Chequamegon. Yellow pollen smokes above the junipers of the Sangre de Cristos. Along the northern coast of California, vultures soar with gulls out over mustard-covered ridges. In the grass below, a pungent odor announces that mother skunk is abroad.

We like to think that spring comes in straight and steady, but it seldom does. In colder climes, the thaw begins. Rivulets form and rush to make a stream. Toads and turtles break their sleep, and fish that languished on the bottom rise in warming lakes. Then a snowfall sets the season back. The stream must wait; ice reclaims the lake. These worst days dampen the spirit, making us wonder if winter ever will be over.

But the snow does melt, the stream expands, and turtles waken. Now the days are jovial and fresh. Spring's zesty air is heady stuff, and we, like the rest of nature, go just a little mad. In homes and offices that don't admit the smells and calls and sights of spring, we get fidgety like hungry rattlesnakes emerging from their winter dens. We must be out! We must touch and taste the world of spring as surely as the rattlesnake must have its meal.

Before long come days that give a glimpse of summer's fullness. Offering heat and light beyond spring's normal quotient, these days start and end in coolness. Their heat invigorates, but does not burden us.

March has no manners, and April easily forgets them. By April, though, the country basks in warmer weather. Snow turns to showers, puddles form. Every sunlit day more creatures greet the year. Butterflies and moths and ants appear. By May the year has some decorum. There may be one last surprise, one last bid for winter; but it is almost summer on the desert and full spring beside the lakes of Michigan. Along the Klamath, the bobcat and the otter have young to feed. This season is drawing to its end. There comes a moment in every life when we know we're grown and there's no going back. That's the way of June.

Spring reawakens us to life and all it means. Walking down a country lane among the butterflies and birds and fresh-greened trees, we are no different from other forms of life. Like them, we feel the season's throb and quicken to its pace.

Days begin to warm, and soil responds. Before long, the humble night gardener uncoils in its winter burrow and contemplates its chores. The earthworm makes its way to the surface for a meal. But it is shy, even in the darkness, and while it looks for withered leaves, it keeps its tail firmly anchored in its tunnel, for it knows there are other hungry souls about.

Family: Lumbricidae   *Genus: Lumbricus*
Species: terrestris

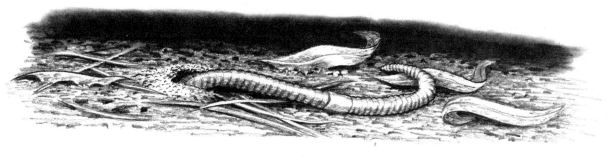

When willows bloom and melted snows turn the
bog to soggy peat, a furry black-gold bumblebee awakes.
Responding to spring's urgings, the queen sips nectar
and dusts rich pollen from her hairy face. Then, sleek
and full, she searches for a burrow where she can build
her nest and bear her young. This first brood will be her
most demanding, for she must raise them all alone.
Once she's found a spot that suits her, the queen builds
and fills a honeypot to sustain her through her brood-
ing. Then she lays her eggs and spreads her abdomen
over them. There she stays until the eggs hatch, leaving
only briefly each day to feed and refill her honeypot for
the night ahead.

Family:Apidae   Genus:Bombus
Species:pennsylvanicus pennsylvanicus

April is a topsy-turvy month, which the night sky
gracefully illustrates: as Leo takes its place in the
heavens, the Big Dipper turns on its head and spills into
the Little Dipper just below.

Beneath the gravel of swift-running western streams, tiny salmon eggs lay still and safe all winter. With spring's first breath, minute larvae emerge from their cases but don't leave their rocky nest quite yet. Too weak to be safe, they are still attached to their yolk-sacs. Day by day they grow stronger. The ice breaks up as the water warms, and food is plentiful in the stream above. After the sacs wither, mouths open, and the infants take on the form of adult sockeyes. When all the changes are complete, they wriggle through the gravel and come up to feed.

Family: Salmonidae
Genus: Oncorhynchus
Species: nerka

Spring rains bring puddles in their wake. As low spots fill with water, the chain of life begins. Flying insects come, attracted by reflected light; the wind blows others in. Some life was there already, waiting in the dirt: algae burst their spores, protozoans break their cysts, the fairy shrimp awakes. Now frogs and toads and mosquitoes join the fray during the few days the puddle lives.

Throughout North America, in spruce forests and apple orchards, under dead elms or on new burns, the fruit of a thready soil fungus thrusts its tawny head up through the melting snows of April and May. It is the delectable black morel, earliest of the edibles. In its wrinkled cap, grown dark with age, wait the spores of future springs' delights. When these are ready, the mushroom sends out its progeny in a cloud to colonize the ground.

Family: Morchellaceae
Genus: Morchella
Species: elata

Ambling through the eons like some comic character, the opossum is North America's most primitive mammal, with its brood pouch, its fifty teeth and other oddities. Perhaps its most extraordinary traits affect its courtship. When a male mounts a female, the two fall over. If they fall to the right, copulation occurs; if they fall to the left, mating is much less likely. When they do mate, the male leaves a plug inside the female to keep her chaste. In about thirty-six hours the plug falls out. If the female isn't pregnant, she can mate again.

Family: Didelphidae
Genus: Didelphus
species: virginianus

Oceans also feel the surge of spring. Off Georgia's coast, each day grows four seconds longer until there is daylight enough to divide the one-celled ocean plants called diatoms. These rootless wanderers split, then split again, so rapidly that in a single day the water's winter blue turns to soft ochre. In another day a myriad of larval animals rise from cold aquatic depths to graze upon this drifting meadow. The sea is thick with life: babies of barnacles, shrimps and clams and hosts of nomad plants. This composite is called plankton. It will be the food of the ocean's many grazers, from feather-duster worms to baleen whales.

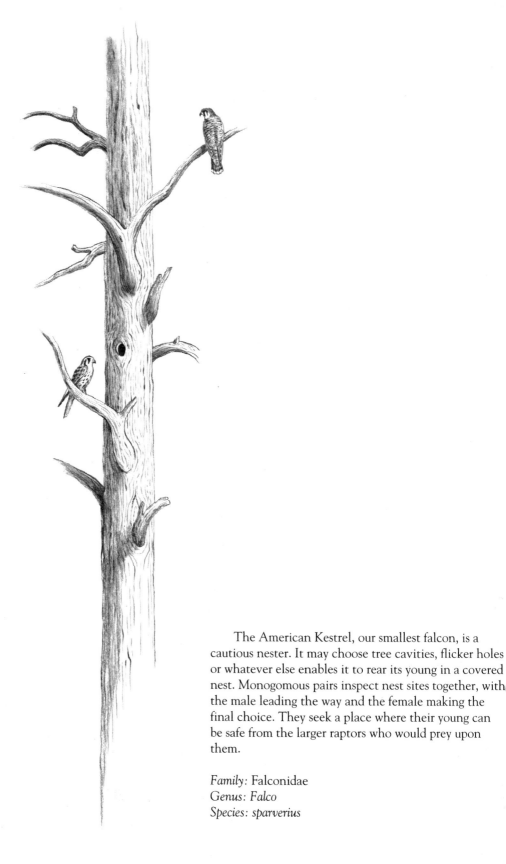

The American Kestrel, our smallest falcon, is a cautious nester. It may choose tree cavities, flicker holes or whatever else enables it to rear its young in a covered nest. Monogomous pairs inspect nest sites together, with the male leading the way and the female making the final choice. They seek a place where their young can be safe from the larger raptors who would prey upon them.

Family: Falconidae
Genus: Falco
Species: sparverius

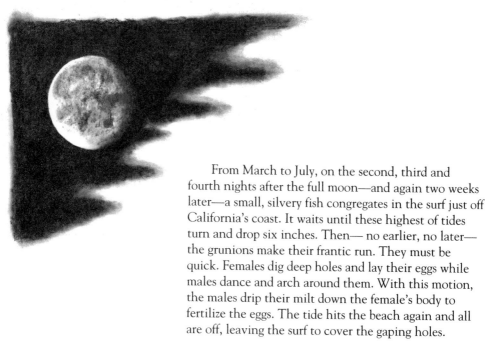

From March to July, on the second, third and fourth nights after the full moon—and again two weeks later—a small, silvery fish congregates in the surf just off California's coast. It waits until these highest of tides turn and drop six inches. Then— no earlier, no later— the grunions make their frantic run. They must be quick. Females dig deep holes and lay their eggs while males dance and arch around them. With this motion, the males drip their milt down the female's body to fertilize the eggs. The tide hits the beach again and all are off, leaving the surf to cover the gaping holes.

Family: Atherinidae   *Genus: Leuresthes*
Species: tenuis

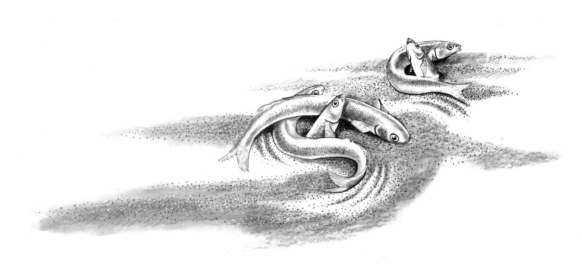

Eating is the first order of caterpillar life, and tent caterpillars begin when their favorite trees start to bud. As they wander about, eating, infant caterpillars unfurl their silken thread, until a tent surrounds them, protecting them from springtime's moody temperament. As they grow larger, the young caterpillars wander off to feed, but return to the tent to rest and digest their food.

Family: Lasiocampidae
Genus:Malacosoma
Species:americanum

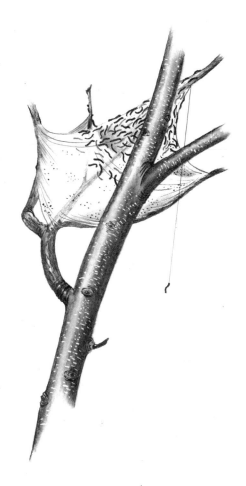

When plants first moved out of the oceans and onto land, new ways to deliver sperm to waiting eggs were needed. Early plants, like modern ferns, relied on a wet environment to bring the two together. But as the land grew drier, fine, powdery pollen evolved. This change allowed plants to colonize vast new reaches of the planet. Over time, nature developed a variety of ways to move pollen through air.

Conifers and grasses use wind to carry their pollen to others of their kind. Some of these species (like the southeastern shortleaf pine and a few of its relatives) have developed female conelets aerodynamically designed to snare the matching pollen, which often must travel hundreds of miles to find its mate. As it does, we curse it, for it is the wind pollinators that cause us the sneezing and the itchy eyes of spring.

Family: Pinaceae *Genus:Pinus*
Species: echinata

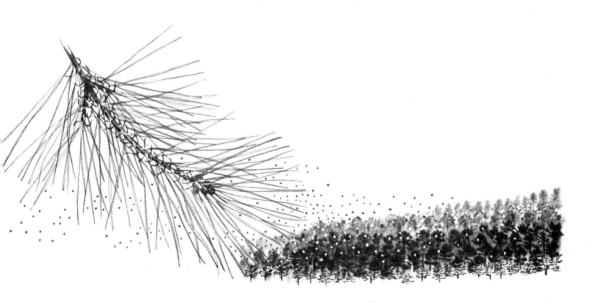

Some plants pollinate themselves. In early spring, a blue violet lifts its head through dark, damp soil. Heart-shaped leaves and purple flowers rise on fragile stalks. If there are other violets nearby, insects will pollinate its flowers. But just in case it bloomed alone, the provident violet flowers again. These buds are inconspicuous and don't open. Inside, the stamens, or male parts, and the pistil, the female part, come in contact with one another. Pollen catches on the sticky surface of the pistil and the flower pollinates itself. Then it sends out a mass of clones to start the cycle once again.

Family: Violaceae   *Genus: Viola*
Species: adunca

In May, as spring draws to a close on the Sonoran desert, a small, brown bat returns to its summer home just as the great cacti begin to bloom. When the flowers open each evening, about an hour after sunset, the bats lap up the waiting nectar, getting pollen grains all over their furry heads and faces. Thus, the long-nosed, nectar-loving bat pollenates the giant saguaros, organ pipes and other cacti.

Family: Phyllostomatidae
Genus: Leptonycteris
Species: sanborni

SUMMER

Summer comes crowned with light and robed in heat. For some of us it is a haughty, despotic ruler; for others it is friendly, benevolent. Whatever else, summer plays counterpoint to winter. Where winter is the gentle season, summer beats down in harsh betrayal; where winter offers the cruelest months, summer brings life and hope and ripe fulfillment.

Summer means bright beginnings, blue and warm. It means dawns that stretch almost to bursting and dusks that do likewise as the sun lingers past its setting. Everywhere the sun defines itself in the straighter, shorter shadows it casts. Still, a change in latitudes offers different flavors to the season. Across the plains, skies untarnished by a cloud in morning soon choke with moisture that will refuse to fall as rain. In the Everglades, days are bathed in steamy dampness. On the Mojave, a stark, parched landscape takes any cover it can, to await another season. Bold summer doesn't question its identity. If a year is a metaphor for the seasons of a life, then summer is full grown, mature.

Perhaps the insects best understand the cadence of this time, for all through our land they sound the songs of industry as they hasten to their tasks. Bees and wasps and dragonflies prefer the hottest time of day, while most mammals—like rabbits and coyotes—prefer to linger under shady trees until the air is cooler.

Evenings may be oppressively hot—or, after bracing showers, fragrant and refreshing. Mosquitoes rise above a pond, gnats and midges swarm. Swallows streak through simmered air, then nighthawks ply their trade. Bats swoop and dive through the deepening darkness. Finally, animals that slept all day begin to stir; foxes, mice and rattlesnakes prefer to seek their living in the night.

The burgeoning days of June build toward the summer solstice until the sun stands longest in the sky. After that the days begin, imperceptibly, to shrink again. For the Sonoran desert, this is the hottest month; in Vermont the greatest warmth is yet to come. By July every creature has caught the rhythm of the season. Even late-nesting birds have gotten to their work, while those who got an early start are feeding hungry nestlings. August skies are alive with shooting stars, and the sun that roused us early just a month ago now lets us sleep a while longer. Dawn and dusk have also shortened, but the earth has built a store of heat and it will be some time before we feel the change.

At last, September brings its coppery glow to summer's waning face. As shadows lengthen and the earth takes on a different hue, we turn our thoughts to fall.

The calendar may not admit to summer, but when fireflies flicker in the evening air, the season has begun. Other insects can produce light, but only fireflies flash distinct signals. They blink most on warm, moist, moonless nights; these flashes lead the males to females waiting in the grass. The system isn't all romance, though. In at least one species, the mated glowworm adapts her signal to attract males of other species; when they alight, she promptly eats them!

Family: Lampyridae
Genus: Photuris
Species: pennsylvanica

The expression "busy as a bee" couldn't be more accurate. To make a pound of honey, a bee must visit *fifty thousand* flowers, and a hive uses *one hundred pounds* or more each winter! When several species of flowers are blooming, honeybees must work smart as well as hard. Each bee chooses one species and collects only that pollen and nectar. Older, experienced bees choose difficult plants that offer the greatest rewards, while young bees harvest the easier ones.

Family: Apidae   *Genus:* Apis
Species: mellifera

The Monterey salamander
looks like easy prey, but it has
an ingenious defense. It produces a thick liquid at the base
of its fatty tail. Should a garter
snake threaten, the salamander
doesn't run. Instead, it turns its
back on the attacker, stands
stiff-legged and sway-backed; as
the snake moves closer, the
salamander arches its tail and
strikes. If its strike is true, the
unfortunate snake finds his
mouth glued shut, all hope of a
meal vanished. The salamander
then departs.

Family: Plethontidae
Genus: Ensatidina
Species: eschscholtzi

Family: Colubridae
Genus: Thamnophis
Species: sirtalis

Just as cold temperatures require biological adaptations, so summer heat triggers innate responses. Cormorants, for example, breed and nest in large colonies called shaggeries, off both coasts and on inland lakes, where they cope with days of relentless summer heat. Like other bird species, they have developed an unusual way to force heat from their bodies by opening their mouths wide and vibrating the thin expandable gular membranes. Fluttering the sac increases the blood supply to the throat and increases the birds' featherless surface area. Blood loses heat as it flows through these exposed areas, speeding heat loss.

Family: Phalacrocoracidae
Genus: Phalacrocorax   *Species:auritus*

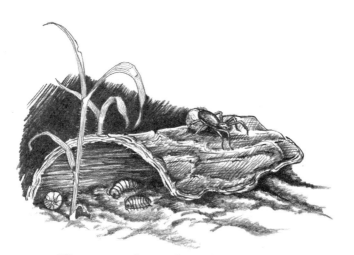

Warming weather can bring
out the best in mothers, even
creepy-crawly ones like rolly
pollies or spiders. Rolly pollies
carry their eggs in a pouch much
as opossums and kangaroos carry
their babies. Wolf spiders make
a silk egg sac, then attach it to
their abdomen and carry it
about. When the tiny spider-
lings hatch, they climb onto the
mother's back and stay there for
several days.

Family: Armadillidae
Genus: Armadillidium
Species: vulgare

Family: Lycosidae
Genus: Lycosa
Species: tarsalis

While the neighbors of the eastern ruby-throated hummingbird build their makeshift nests of grass and twigs, this tiny bird dines on nectar and frolics in the flowerbeds. But she's no fool; every craftsman demands the proper tools. To form her nursery, she must have spider's silk, lichen and fluffy down from the cinnamon fern. When the summer offers all of these, and only then, will she go to work. The fern's fluff will make a thick felt lining for the nest, the spider's silk will cover it and the gray-green lichen will camouflage her treasure.

Family: Trochilidae   *Genus: Archilochus*
Species: colubris

The spadefoot toad is utterly dependent on moisture to live and reproduce, yet it lives where rain is always scarce, and breeding ponds exist only a few days each year. To meet these harsh demands, this small toad spends most of the year in underground burrows, dug with its spaded hind feet. The tiny, black "shovels" allow it to dig down to permanently damp soil. There the toad waits until rain comes. But how do spadefoots, deep in their dark parlors, know it is raining? Do they hear it or smell it, even twenty feet beneath the surface?

Family: Pelobatidae
Genus: Scaphiopus
Species: bombifrons

The very sound of the word cicada lends summer's cadence to a poet's work. That insistent hum comes from males calling other males to converge and display themselves to females. While most insect musicians fiddle (by rubbing two body parts together), the cicada is a drummer. The last segment of his thorax houses two hollow cavities covered on one side with membranes that act as tiny drumheads; attached to these are muscles the cicada moves to make the drumskin rattle.

Family: Cicadidae
Genus: Tibicen
Species: canicularis

Perhaps our country's oddest mammal is the nine-banded armadillo. A recent immigrant from South America, it is probably our only July breeding mammal. But this is hardly the strangest thing about this armored creature. More surprising is the fact that it produces four identical offspring. Females regularly produce only one egg, which is fertilized by a single sperm; but the egg splits into four, giving the armadillo mother her lookalike quadruplets.

Family: Daypodidae   *Genus: Dasypus*
Species: novemcinctus

Summer wends along. Many birds begin a second clutch, some even leave for southern parts. But the merry goldfinch takes no notice of the time. It's late, we call to her, for she hasn't even built a nest. Just when all seems lost, the thistle bursts its spiny bracts and offers seeds and airy down. The goldfinch stops cavorting. Eager now, she carts away the soft, white down to make her thick-walled nest. She eats the seed. Soon a healthy brood of young eat as well. The growing goldfinch family may eat ten thousand seeds a day! Wisely, this savvy little bird waited for her bountiful harvest.

Family: Fringillidae
Genus: Carduelis
Species: tristis

Dragonflies are an ancient, still-thriving insect group. The white-tailed dragonfly, our most common species, is found hovering over ponds and streams at the height of summer. Males are easiest to spot because they return to the same perchs each day to wait for the females, who come to water only to breed, lay eggs and drink. Males compete for preferred spots but avoid outright combat by signaling their status to one another. A dominant male raises his abdomen and displays its whitened underside.

Family: Libellulidae   *Genus: Plathemis*
Species: lydia

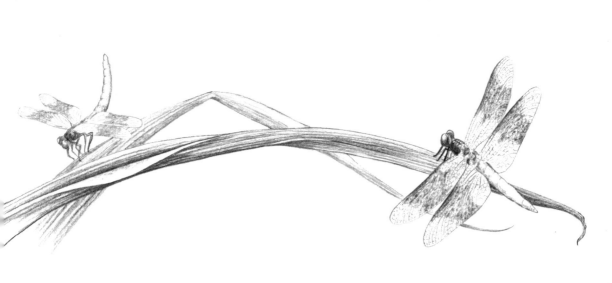

Summer storms bring drama to the landscape.
Across the West, lightning splits hot afternoons apart,
thunder slaps the air and rain falls to grant a brief relief.
Growing banks of cumulus clouds warn of incipient
thunderheads. These woolly clouds thicken and gather
moisture until they form flat anvil heads; only then do
they dump their gift in drenching sheets or a steady,
pattering downpour.

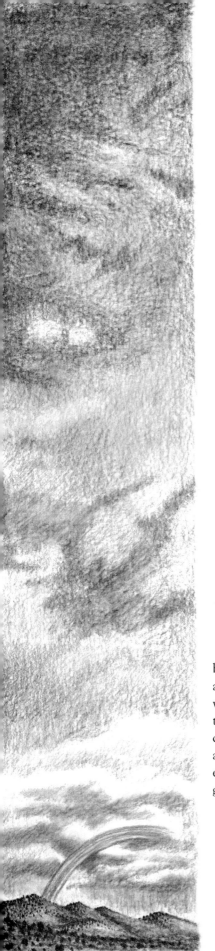

Sometimes summer rain offers a softer side. Rainbows are a winsome mixture of sunlight and raindrops and their interraction with the human eye. Nothing less will do. Sunlight enters bubble-shaped raindrops at just the right angle to bend and separate into its many colors. These colors then hit the back of the raindrop and are reflected forward again. As they emerge, our eyes see the seven hues: red on top, then orange, yellow, green, blue, indigo and, finally, violet.

The beach looks tranquil on hot afternoons, yet marauders haunt its rocky pools. Starfish creep ponderously about on adhesive feet. For all their slow advance, these echinoderms wreak havoc on huge populations of their favorite meal. It must be the crazy way they eat. They use their feet to pry open mussel shells, then insert their stomachs inside out into the hapless mollusks. Stomach juices break down the mussels' soft bodies, and the starfish suck in the gooey mixture. Then they lumber on to their next unwitting prey.

Family: Asteriidae   *Genus: Asterias*
Species: forbesi
Family: Mytildae   *Genus: Mytilus*
Species: edulis

We may laugh as the tiny
fiddler crab waves its oversized
claw in time to a music we can't
hear, but this hearty soul has
made its home in an envi-
ronment of great extremes.
Much like deserts, tidal estuaries
demand great survival skills of
their inhabitants. The fiddler
crab and its neighbors daily con-
front drowning and dehydra-
tion, overheating on parched
beaches, sudden cold waters and
drastic changes in salinity. To
protect themselves, crabs use
burrows. They are able to
anticipate tides and are uncanny
in their ability to find their way
along featureless mudflats.

Family: Ocypedidae
Genus: Uca
Species: minax

The second week of August brings the Perseid showers. Meteors streak across the sky. Most appear near the constellation Perseus, then draw their fiery tails over Casseopeia and the Big Dipper. Each rushing meteor enters our atmosphere at about twenty miles a second. It becomes luminous at a height of about sixty miles, and then, as a rule, vanishes, burned out, forty miles away.

As summer slips from the prairie, big bluestem fades from green to gold and brown. Through June, July and August, this giant grass defied heat, pelting rains and drying winds. By growing tall and dense, it created a cool, damp microclimate near its base that nourished its vast root system. But summer fades, and stalks that towered over the land begin to wither. Brittle stems fall, then crumble and, in time, replenish the land.

Family: Gramineae   *Genus: Andropogon*
Species: gerardi

AUTUMN

Autumn is a bit like spring: alive with energy and change. There's a bustle in the air as days grow short. Like spring, autumn offers promise, but with an added depth, for now the year looks back farther than it looks ahead.

Early autumn days are not so different from the ones just past: the sun still warms, leaves still hold their green, the sky is still an uncompromising blue. But through September autumn gathers strength. In the Rocky Mountains the air is crisp, nighttime temperatures plunge then bounce back at the sun's most gentle prodding.

Those creatures that cannot last the winter waste little time on food. Instead, they rush to leave behind the seeds of another generation. Crickets call long and ardently, then lay their eggs in sheltered spots for spring to find. Having done their work, they make their peace. For those who'll greet the spring in different form, the tasks are two: to eat enough to last the winter and to form cocoons to protect them from the elements and hide their metamorphosis. Throughout the East, caterpillars of the cecropia moth seek out sturdy twigs to act as anchor for their cocoons.

Along the Rogue River, anxious goslings take their final flying lessons. Nearby, mother mergansers stress take-off etiquette to gawky ducklings. Then one day, the pond is bare of ducks, the river still. The summer crew is gone and we are left behind. Now comes a pause when the world holds its breath, waiting for the grip of winter. We gather wood, pull warm clothes from closets and harvest fields of bounty.

September toys with change as it mimics summer. It is the time of early-turning trees and rich, ripe berries. Even so, the golden-mantled ground squirrel has taken to its den. October is a month of contrast—red and gold against the green, cold nights back to back with still-warm days. Streams are cooling back and heavy-headed grasses sway on brown-gold stalks. By November the year tries on its winter garb for fit. Days are short, nights cold. The pungent scents of decaying leaves and woodsmoke fill the air.

Autumn is nostalgia's time. Air shimmers. Leaves tumble whispering to earth. We can't escape the message: the outdoor world is fit and fat, but death is close behind. Even so, we feel the glory of this season, still full of vigor, yet serene.

Across the Rocky Mountains, wapiti calls the autumn. His is the song of September in the high country. Sleek and fat, his head heavy with antlers, the bull elk prepares to amass his harem. But his orgy will cost him dearly. Afterward, spent and gaunt, he must eat well, quickly, to survive the winter. Still, each year he chances it, for he will have his moment.

Family: Cervidae   *Genus: Cervus*
Species: canadensis

About September 23, earth
and sun stand at the autumn
equinox. The sun's rays hit
earth exactly perpendicular to
the equator. The short days of
winter are beginning for the
northern hemisphere and just
ending for its southern counter-
part. For this brief moment, the
hours of day and night are equal
everywhere on the planet.

Gazing into the dark universe isn't for the faint of
heart. The brightest stars are gone now, but the Milky
Way is dense in autumn's sky and its galaxies add luster
to the night. The Great Galaxy of Andromeda, the
nearest to our own, is the most distant light we can see
with our naked eye. This light must awe and humble us,
for it has traveled over two million years to reach our
corner of the universe.

Days grow cool and the sun recedes. Now crickets call and listen for their kind. Their songs will lead them to their mates. These musical insects have sensitive hearing—even though their ears are on their front knees!

Family: Gryllida *Genus: Acheta* *Species: assimilis.*

By late summer, ground
squirrels eat voraciously. Before
long, other winter sleepers follow suit. Brown bats, wood-
chucks and bears all feel the
urge to lay on stores of fat. The
true hibernators feast until
they've had enough, then they
fast briefly to clear their bodies
of wastes. Many eat foods that
cause a body plug to form. Only
then do their bodies cool down,
their hearts and breathing slow.
Their deep sleep begins.

*Family:*Sciuridae
Genus: Spermophillus
Species: tridecemlineatus

High on rocky outcrops
where limestone cracks and
caves in upon itself, sinkholes
form. These limestone chambers
are the favored winter resting
grounds for garter snakes.
Solitary all summer, they now
slither together toward the
sinkholes in great hordes to
sleep away the winter.

*Family:*Colubridae
Genus:Thamnophis
Species:sirtalis parietalis

Unlike animals, plants must stand their ground against the changing season. Deciduous trees drop their leaves and retreat into themselves. Before they do, if the weather has been bright and cool but not too cold, they may offer a grand display. The show happens after a narrow ring of tissue forms at the base of each aging leaf stem. This ring of cells chokes off the flow of nutrients into and out of the leaf. Green chlorophyll fades and newly made glucose is trapped in the dying leaf. The oranges and yellows that lay hidden beneath the green show themselves. In trees that produce lots of glucose, vivid reds appear.

Family: Aceraceae   *Genus: Acer*
Species: rubrum

As autumn draws on, the broadwing begins its journey south. This is a small hawk, but a heavy, lumbering bird, not well-suited to long flight. Yet it travels nearly fifty-five hundred miles to winter in Columbia. The broadwing manages not so much by brute force as by an uncanny ability to judge and use weather, flying only on days perfect for the task. The hawk rides thermals over flat country or catches lift along ridges, then glides for miles. Although often in the company of many hawks, sometimes even thousands, using the same air space, the broadwing always flys alone.

Family: Accipitridae
Genus: Buteo
Species: platypterus

The monarch butterfly also responds to cooling days by journeying over two thousand miles. Monarchs, with a top cruising speed of twelve miles an hour, would die long before reaching their destination if they relied solely on their tiny wings. Instead, like hawks, they fly the thermals, catch lift and sometimes fly at altitudes of several thousand feet.

Family: Danaidae   *Genus: Danaus*
Species:plexippus

Summer is gone, and man retreats into autumn's endeavors. Finally the beaches of our coasts breathe free again, and it is time to wander quietly along the deserted, sandy shores. A harsh place of few resources, this habitat is replenished by treasures thrust up by the tide. The ragged necklace of kelp and shells and detritus is the strandline— high tide's gift, home to sandhoppers, food to all sorts of beach dwellers.

Autumn means abrupt independence and harsh reality to many of summer's young. In territorial species like red squirrels, the change brings chattering, irritated outbursts from the elders. Red squirrel mothers are not sentimental: at weaning time, they simply carry their young to a new territory and leave them to fend for themselves, or else they move away and leave the young behind. The little ones must hurry to find a place to live, learn what's edible and store provisions for the winter.

Family: Sciuridae   *Genus:* Tamiasciurus
Species: hudsonicus

Goldenrod galls are plump and round long before October. Inside, the gall fly larva is hard at work. It will retire soon, but first it must complete an escape hatch for spring. To do this, the larva chews into the gall's soft tissue, leaving only a thin film of skin on the outside. In spring, after it has pupated into a fly, it rams the door to make its exit.

Family: Tephritidae
Genus: Eurosta
Species: solidaginis

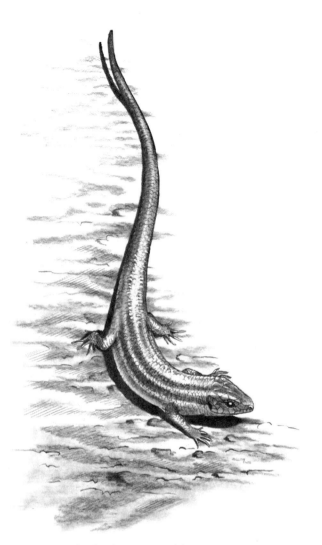

As the days grow colder, the muscles of cold-blooded animals work more slowly; everything takes longer. Like other lizards, the five-lined skink will go underground to stay the winter. But for now it basks in the sun for long periods, putting its body at right angles to the sun's rays and spreading out to catch the warmth. If it gets too warm, the skink orients itself parallel to the sun and draws in its body.

Family: Scincidae
Genus: Eumeces
Species: fasciatus

It is along the margins of habitats like those where trees and grasses meet that life abounds. Here the plants of forest and field intermix; so, too, the animals. But there are other species not found in either habitat that choose this unique terrain as home. Walk here in autumn's bustle, and the harvest will be rich indeed.

The arctic sun falls so
swiftly that each October day
may be twenty minutes shorter
than the last. In the waning
daylight, pregnant polar bears
move inland from the pack ice
to dig out ample dens. Here they
will snooze away the time of
their confinement. Others hunt
all through the winter, but these
females won't emerge again
until their cubs are ready to
explore their arctic homeland.

Family: Ursidae
Genus: Thalarctos
Species: maritimus

The leaves are off the beeches. For a while they skim the surface of a stream, then, decaying, fall to the bottom. There amid the rubble, stonefly nymphs, newly hatched, eat their way through the feast. In the silent, rotting litter, one of the planet's great energy transfers takes place. What the stonefly leaves, the caddisfly may eat. What the caddisfly can't use, something else will prize. Tomorrow a trout will take the nymph, then you or I will take the trout.

Family: Fagaceae
Genus: Fagus
Species: grandifolia

The brown bear has slipped into its den, the caribou have resolved their conflicts, the crickets are gone. Yet as earth and sun move toward their appointment with the winter solstice, manatees frolic in our southern waters. Winter has no harsh words for this gentle mammal, who mates even in December. Winter frames the country; for many its grip is tight already. But there is renewal in an ending, and the manatee whispers that the cycle of the seasons suits the changing needs of its many creatures.

Family: Trichechidae   *Genus: Trichechus*
Species: manatus

WINTER

Winter's image is a vivid one. Yet the days of winter are not at all alike. Some dawn clear and piercing, blessed with a crystal sharpness that is numbed by heat in summer. Some offer mists that enshroud the landscape and hold us distant from every living thing; on these days we can only hope that we are not alone. Still other days are leaden and bear a granite weight to our souls. We are grateful when these pass and we feel again the cheer a clearing sky admits.

In some regions, winter rages. In others, it is benign, offering freedom from the tyranny of summer heat. In the northern reaches of the country, winter is the harshest season. In humid Georgia and the Carolinas, it is a time of relief. Depending on the latitude, we feel the urge to hole up in a warm place or to amble out across a resting, silent landscape. We see winter as the fallow time. It is a metaphor for death.

Whether on the desert or in the high mountains, the telling signs of winter's coming are lower temperatures and shorter days. Our planet lives by a slender thread that balances solar energy within the narrow range we earthbound creatures can accept. Winter takes us to the coldest, darkest point. How dark and how cold depends on how far north we live. It begins sometime in autumn. The difference builds as days fall in upon themselves: dawn and dusk and the day between grow shorter as we approach the winter solstice. The shortest day, December 21, marks the official start of winter.

By January the days have begun to open out again. At first the signs are subtle, too small to see. January may be fierce or bleak, but through the month, light pushes back the edges of the night. February offers what it can to winter's bag of tricks. In its harshest, coldest storms, it sometimes seems that there is only dusk, no real day at all. In spite of that, the days grow on. It's March before we sense the end of winter. March goes from cold to warm and back again, then repeats the pattern, sometimes in hours rather than in days. Even with its fits and starts, there's no question now: spring is in the offing.

Winter is a time exposed. Trees and shrubs reveal their naked skeletons. We house dwellers assume there's nothing going on in winter, that all forms of life outdoors are hiding from the season. But take a walk and a myriad of questions form: What bird is singing, hidden in the tree? Who made those fresh tracks in the snow? Did a cottontail crop that grass? Which winds bring the fiercest storms? To the sharp eye, the willing ear, winter's quiet secrets unfold, and we take strength from the meditation that is an open, silent meadow.

Seasons are caused by the differential heating of the earth's surface. On December 21, the day we call the winter solstice ("sun standing still"), sunlight falls directly on the Tropic of Capricorn. For a moment, the sun appears to hesitate, then swings slowly back to retrace its route. With this, the southern hemisphere experiences its longest day, the northern its longest night. Now winter claims sovereignty over all lands north of the equator.

The brilliant winter sky is heralded in by the December arrival of the constellation Orion. The Hunter rules the sky now, with Sirius and Taurus at its flanks. Sirius, by far the brightest star, is easy to find in its position 25 degrees southeast of the three unmistakable stars of Orion's belt. Now man, lonely in the long nights, whispers tales of bravery and comfort across the winter darkness.

The great horned owl is North America's earliest nester. By braving February's freezing temperatures, this owl is best able to provide for its young. Hunting is easiest in late winter and early spring, when trees and brush are bare and there is little cover to protect the owlets' favored food item, the cottontail. By late April, when owlets are growing fast, female cottontails have young of their own and must forage longer than usual, leaving themselves open to more exposure. Hence, just as seed- and insect-eating birds time their breeding season to coincide with peak food availability, so too does the great horned owl.

Family: Strigidae   *Genus: Bubo*
Species: virginianus

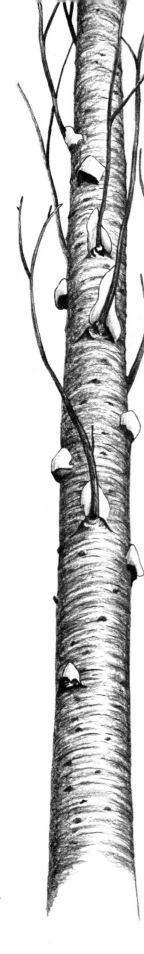

The needle-like shape and long life of conifer leaves give evergreens certain advantages in harsh habitats. Trees like pines and firs are able to withstand hot summers, cold winters and harsh mountain winds. The design of conifer needles cuts water loss, so these trees are able to keep their leaves through winter. Thus, they can continue photosynthesis, while broadleafed, deciduous neighbors like the aspen stand dormant.

Family: Pinaceae   *Genus: Pinus*
Species: edulis

Family: Salicaceae   *Genus: Populus*
Species: tremuloides

Most creatures that inhabit snow country survive by making use of snow's physical properties. Because heat doesn't move well through snow, it acts as a thick layer of insulation, so, strange as it may seem, those creatures that live under this blanket are more apt to survive than those who live above it, especially in bad winters. Snow is also wonderful construction material and all sorts of small animals—shrews, voles and gophers—construct tunnels and runways in it so that they can move about freely.

Pikas are among the most industrious of the winter snow dwellers. In early fall they chew off fragments of grasses and sedges, leaving them in small piles like haystacks to dry. This harvest will feed them through the winter. Pikas live only in rocky talus slopes, where extensive chambers and tunnels provide comfortable housing and storage places for their crop. In their roomy abodes, they are safe from the harsh winter climate that rages on the mountaintop above.

Family: Ochotonidae   *Genus: Ochotona*
Species: princeps

Soils are the product of an ongoing process called weathering. When geological materials such as granite become exposed, the forces of water, wind and temperature break them into smaller and smaller fragments over the course of time. As seasons shift, repeated freezing and thawing create an abundance of these forces. While it takes centuries to make soil from mountains, we can observe the many stages of the process in certain areas, such as a mountain canyon: a granite wall shows cracks and fissures in its many faces, while, on the ground, fallen boulders sit. The rocks and gravel that fan out from the base of a mountain give testimony to the fact that all things bow to the relentless power of the elements.

A granite boulder is an unlikely spot for a baby pine; yet there it is, small but hopeful. How did it come to be there? The process begins when lichen gains a foothold in a craggy fissure or a rough surface. Lichen take nutrients from air and rain water, and sometimes directly from the surface on which they grow. Through time they etch the rock, and dusty particles get trapped in the lichen's coarse web. As mosses move in, the lichen disappears, unsuited to the environment it has created. A thin soil gradually accumulates, in which a young ponderosa or a tiny apache plume may take root. Whatever the new plant may be, it will be the result of a lengthy and resolute natural process.

Family: Pinaceae *Genus: Pinus*
Species: ponderosa

Earning a living in winter can be difficult. Some species adjust to hard times by changing their diets; acorn woodpeckers, though, like all good investors, accommodate by working to save for a rainy day. While food is plentiful, they cache it, using tree trunks, telephone poles, even fenceposts to store their nuts. Where the food souce is predictable and storage facilities are good, these birds become territorial, and the whole family protects its investment. The best of these terrritories pass from generation to generation, just as inheritances do among people.

Family: Picidae
Genus: Melanerpes
Species: formicivorus

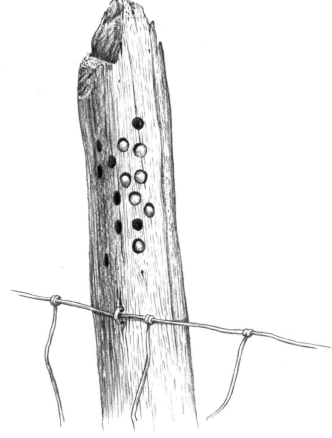

When we think of birds and winter migration, we picture avian travelers moving from north to south over long distances to warm, even tropical, places. But for some, the Pacific Northwest is south enough. The bohemian waxwing, a boreal forest dweller, comes down from Canada and Alaska and considers the northwestern United States a hospitable winter home.

Family: Bombycillidae   *Genus: Bombycilla*
Species: garrulus

Farther south, the gray-headed junco carries out vertical migration, moving from a high elevation to a lower one. In the mountain areas of the West, it is often quite sufficient to move only a few miles downslope to find a more favorable climate.

Family: Fringillidae   *Genus: Junco*
Species: hyemalis

Snowy Owl

Irruption is an intermittent form of migration practiced by some northern birds that have narrow food requirements. "Flight years" occur when the special food source of one of these species suffers a cyclical decline. Most irruptive birds are residents of the tundra or boreal forest: waxwings, crossbills and the snowy owl. Affected birds move from north to south, from higher to lower elevation, from east to west, even from south to north as food availability requires.

Family: Strigidae   *Genus: Nyctea*
Species: scandiaca

There are a number of bird species that do not migrate at all. Not surprisingly, the majority are birds like the Tricolored heron, which inhabits the southern coastal regions of the country. Winter conditions for many of these birds are not unlike those enjoyed by their neighbors in Central and South America.

Family: Ardeidae   *Genus: Egretta*
Species: tricolor

Louisiana Heron

All looks quiet on the frozen surface of lakes and
ponds. But what of the frigid world below? How do
creatures survive in the ice-cold water? Some, like the
beaver and the muskrat, carry on as usual. Their thick
fur, fat bodies and well-wrought homes allow them to
withstand the hardships of winter. Bass and perch
migrate to warmer water at the bottom, where they
move as little as possible. Insect nymphs and larvae
attach to vegetation and sleep away the winter, while
snapping turtles and frogs dig into the muddy bottom
and go into a type of sleep called torpor.

Antifreeze might seem to be a good example of man's inventiveness, but nature snickers at us, for many ancient creatures endure winter's cold naturally, thanks to this very principle. These are animals that either slow down drastically or sleep away the winter: moth larvae, woodlice, certain spiders, even snapping turtles and some frogs. As temperatures drop, these animals build up stores of glycerol, to protect their organs from freezing. With spring's return, the glycerol breaks down, their thickened body fluids thin and life returns to these adaptable creatures.

Family: Chelydridae
Genus: Chelydra
Species: serpintina

The northern long-tailed weasel, like other mammals that change color in winter, begins to shed its rich brown coat as autumn days grow short. At first the change is evident only around the head or the nape of the neck, but gradually it spreads down the animal's sides and toward its back. While naturalists once believed this resulted from a change in temperature, it is now known that, for mammals, color change is related to the amount of light that falls on their eyes. As northern days shorten, decreased stimulation of the optic nerve affects the pituitary gland, which produces the hormones that trigger shedding of the summer coat. In spring, as days grow longer, the process is reversed. Then our weasel regains its summer suit.

Family: Mustelidae   *Genus: Mustela*
Species: frenata

Like the owl that finds it
easiest to spot and catch its prey
in winter, the naturalist, too,
finds the bare limbs and snowy
paths of winter and early spring
just right for stalking certain
quarry. The birder can locate
and identify nests that were hidden in summer's dense foliage,
while the mammal enthusiast
uses the snow to follow tracks
he or she might not notice in
other seasons.

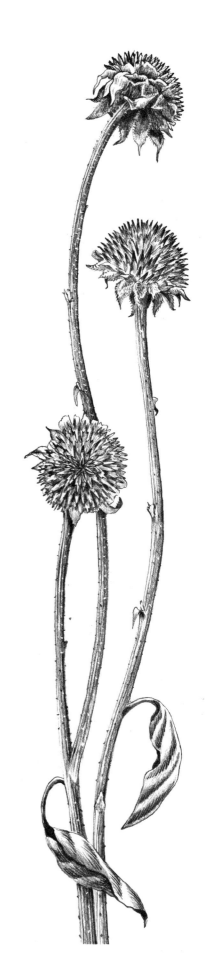

There, proud against the frozen landscape, stands a sunflower skeleton. It is dead, but its work is not yet finished. This is the season of harsh gales and hungry birds. On dry, patient stalks, the prairie sunflower waits, offering its seeds to those who promise to carry them away. And so it is that even winter can be the season of new beginnings.

Family: Compositae
Genus: Helianthus
Species: petiolaris

RESOURCES

FIELD TECHNIQUES

The measure of a good nature walk is not how far you go or how many birds you count but how much you truly see. All kinds of equipment is available to help you learn more about the natural world, from binoculars to field guides to spotting scopes. But before you rely on such devices, begin with the tools you always carry with you—your senses.

Train your eyes to see movement and expand your field of vision. Cup your ears and focus on sounds you may not have noticed before; learn to note the complexity of sounds around you as a musician would. Encourage your sense of smell. Walk up to a tree and sniff the bark; your nose can help you identify many trees this way. Crush a leaf and, closing your eyes, inhale the fresh scent. Concentrate on one sense at a time. Once you have refined these faculties, the world you look at through a hand lens or microscope will be enlarged in more ways than one.

When you go out to observe nature, it's often best to go alone. When we walk with other people, we talk and get distracted; the immediate world is lost on us. Wise hunters and fishermen know the value of a quiet partner; they choose their companions well. Do the same for your own stalking.

Tread lightly. Respect the life around you. The lichen on that boulder you're about to climb may have taken three hundred years to reach its tender size; years of growth could be crushed with one misstep. Watch out for even the mundane bugs. As you learn more about the wonders of insect life, these little creatures won't seem so repugnant or so worthy of extinction. Leave them in their places, so they can show their worlds to you.

One of the first field techniques to learn is how to find the right spot to settle into. This knowledge is often subjective and gets fine-tuned with experience. Once you're comfortable, pull out your notebook and begin taking down your impressions as you feel yourself become part of the setting.

It is valuable to record time, place, temperature and other weather information as you begin an entry. If you are in a place you visit often, it may be interesting to note the time and placement of the sun as it begins to set on this date. If you do this throughout the year, you will become aware of the movement of the sun around your special environment. Such knowledge somehow changes our relationship to the natural world as it becomes familiar to us in a way it was not before.

If you enjoy collecting, do it with a camera or a tape recorder—or your pencil. Don't collect specimens. Man has endangered all manner of species by considering them common and abundant. Taking photographs or recordings are generally acceptable collecting techniques—as are making pictorial or verbal notes in a book such as this. Use this journal/sketchbook to enhance your memory. Record everything that interests you. Make it a habit to look back at past walks from time to time. Gradually, you will see patterns emerge, new mysteries surface. With the revelations that unfold will come a delight you had never before imagined.

RECOMMENDED FIELD GUIDES

There are many wonderful books that are just too bulky to be useful in the field. These volumes are for keeping beside your easy chair, to consult at the end of a day outdoors. They may become well thumbed with time, but they are not take-alongs.

The guides listed here can go in a daypack and be of immediate help in identification. They may not include as much information as the books at home, but they do their job well. Some focus on particular organisms; others, organized by region, cover a broad spectrum of natural history topics. Each has its place. If you carry only one book, take one that is regionally oriented. When you have plenty of room or are looking for just birds or butterflies, for example, the specific field guides will offer more detail.

We recommend the following guides, but this list is only a sampling of what is available.

REGIONAL

Audubon Society Nature Guides. Includes seven regional guides: *The Atlantic and Gulf Coasts, Deserts, Eastern Forests, Grasslands, Pacific Coast, Western Forests,* and *Wetlands.*

Peterson Field Guides. Includes numerous regional field guides dealing with a particular group of organisms. They include: Birds: *Western Birds, Birds of Texas and Adjacent States;* Butterflies: *Western Butterflies, Moths of Eastern North America;* Ferns: *Ferns of Northeastern and Central North America;* Fish: *Pacific Coast Fishes, Atlantic Coast Fishes;* Insects: *Insects of America North of Mexico;* Reptiles and Amphibians: *Reptiles and Amphibians of Eastern and Central North America, Western Reptiles and Amphibians;* Shells: *Shells of the Atlantic and Gulf Coasts and the West*

Indies, Pacific Coast Shells; Wildflowers: *Wildflowers of Northeastern and North Central North America, Southwestern and Texas Wildflowers*

Sierra Club Naturalist's Guides. This series includes guides to the deserts of the Southwest, North Atlantic Coast, North Woods of Michigan, the Sierra Nevada, Southern New England, and the Piedmont. It also includes guides to the natural areas of California; Colorado and Utah; Idaho, Montana and Wyoming; New Mexico, Arizona and Nevada; and Oregon and Washington.

SPECIFIC GUIDES

Birds:

Harrison, Peter. *Seabirds*. Boston: Houghton Mifflin, 1983.

Peterson, Roger Tory. *A Field Guide to Birds*. Peterson Field Guides. Boston: Houghton Mifflin, 1980.

Robbins, Chandler S., Bertel Bruun, and Herbert S. Zim. *A Guide to Field Identification: Birds of North America*. New York: Golden Press, 1966.

Scott, Shirley L., ed. *Field Guide to the Birds of North America*. Washington, D.C.: National Geographic Society, 1988.

Insects:

Arnett, Ross, and Richard Jacques. *Simon and Schuster's Guide to Insects*. New York: Simon and Schuster, 1981.

Borror, Donald J., and Richard E. White. *Insects*. Peterson Field Guides. Boston: Houghton Mifflin, 1970.

Stokes, Donald. *A Guide to Observing Insect Lives*. Boston: Little, Brown and Co., 1983.

White, Richard E. *Field Guide to the Beetles of North America*. Boston: Houghton Mifflin, 1983.

Mammals:

Murie, Olaus J. *A Field Guide to Animal Tracks*. Peterson Field Guides. Boston: Houghton Mifflin, 1975.

Stokes, Donald, and Lillian Stokes. *A Guide to ￼￼￼ and Behavior*. Boston: Little, Brown & Co., 19￼

Whitaker, Jr., John O. *Audubon Society Field ￼￼ can Mammals*. New York: Alfred A. Kn￼

Reptiles and Amphibians:

Behler, John, and F. Wayne King. *Audubon Society Field Guide to North American Reptiles and Amphibians*. New York: Alfred A. Knopf, 1979.

Smith, Hobart M., and Edmund D. Brodie. *A Guide to Field Identification of Reptiles of North America*. New York: Golden Press, 1982.

Stars:

Menzel, Donald H., and Jay M. Pasachoff. *Stars and Planets*. Peterson Field Guides. Boston: Houghton Mifflin.

Trees:

Brockman, C. *Trees of North America*. New York: Golden Press, 1986.

Little, Elbert. *The Audubon Society Field Guide to North American Trees* (2 volumes: Eastern Region and Western Region). New York: Alfred A. Knopf, 1980.

Wildflowers

Newcomb, Lawrence. *Newcomb's Wildflower Guide*. Boston: Little, Brown and Co., 1977.

Niering, William A., and Nancy Olmstead. *Audubon Society Field Guide to North American Wildflowers*. (Eastern Region) .

Spellenberg, Richard. *Audubon Society Field Guide to North American Wildflowers*. (Western Region). New York: Alfred A. Knopf, 1979.

Venning, Frank. *Wildflowers of North America: A Guide to Field Identification*. New York: Golden Press, 1984.

CHECKLIST FOR THE FIELD

Take your eyes, your ears, your nose and, most of all, your questioning mind. With these you always have the essentials for nature watching. Beyond that, a notebook and pencil allow you to record what you see and think. Choose clothing that allows you to fade into the background. The other things on this list are extras, though some may be imperative for a particular trip.

The luxury items can be nice to have along—or they can be nothing more than weight to carry and a means of separating you from the world you want to see. A small portable tape recorder could be of great use when trying to learn to recognize bird songs, but people have been learning these for centuries without such aid. A spotting scope can give you a closer view of all sorts of animals, but it is heavy and you are likely to make noise setting it up. Don't become dependent on gadgets. They have served to separate us from nature far more than they have enhanced it for us.

1. notebook, pencils, waterproof pen
2. daypack
3. field guide(s)
4. binoculars
5. hand lens

Personal Items

6. water
7. Hat
8. sunscreen
9. insect repellant
10. matches
11. walking stick

Extras (including some luxuries)

12. compass
13. topographic maps
14. spotting scope
15. tape measure or ruler
16. field microscope
17. thermometer
18. fisherman's stool
19. camera
20. tape recorder